WHAT IS A WOMAN

WHAT IS A WOMAN

SAM HUMPHREY

samuel c humphrey

v

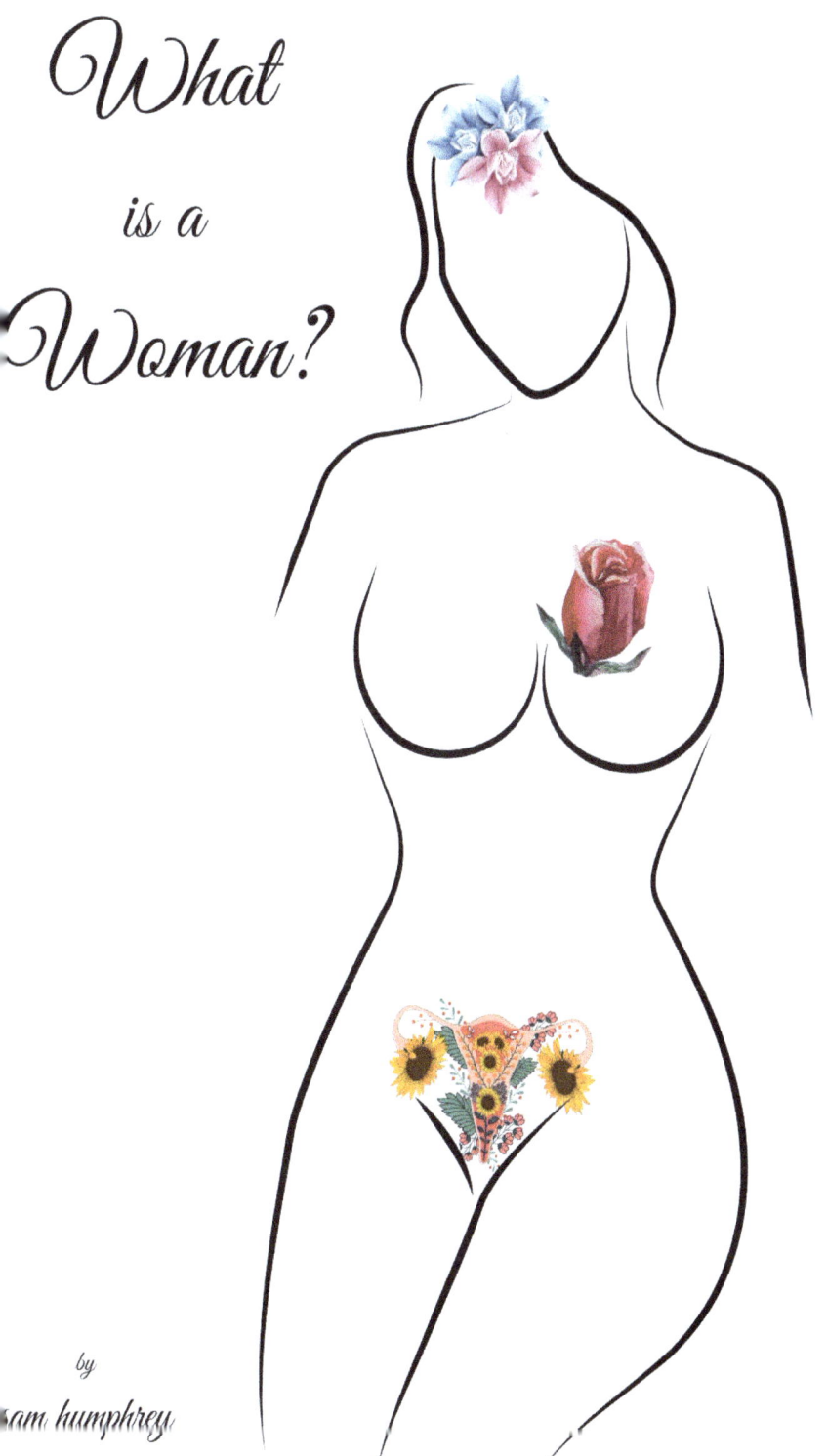

Copyright @ 2023 samuel c humphrey
All rights reserved
sam humphrey 2023
Inspirit Alliance 2023

No part of this book may be reproduced, or stored in a retrieval system, or transmitted in any form or by any means, electronic, mechanical, photocopying, recording, or otherwise, without express written permission of the publisher.

First Edition
e-book ISBN-13: 978-1-959239-06-2
Paperback ISBN-13: 978-1-959239-05-5
Hardback ISBN-13: 978-1-95923908-6
Library of Congress Control Number: 2023903661

Cover design by: sam humphrey
Interior illustrations by: sam humphrey
Dedication and Introduction
illustrations by Anna Berry Jarvis

Printed in the United States of America

Contents

Introduction — xvii

1. Biologically a Woman is: — 3
2. Physically a Woman is: — 7
3. Psychologically a Woman is: — 13
4. But What is a Woman Really? — 19
5. A Degree of Femininity — 25
6. A Woman is Magic — 31

Epilogue — 37

*This Book is Dedicated to
All the Women
of the World*

Introduction

Hello. I am sam humphrey and I am a Human Male – a Man. I used to be a boy, but thanks to the many women in my life I survived, grew, and developed into the man I am now. That starts with my mother and includes my grandmothers, sisters, friends, girlfriends, stepmother, stepsisters, wives, daughter and many others. Without them I wouldn't exist and I wouldn't know how to live, nor would I know what is important in life.

What gives me the Audacity to think I could write a book that answers the question: What is a Woman?

Well, I'll tell you. I was born the first child of four. All three of my siblings are female – that is Women. My mother was a Woman as were both of my Grandmothers. I grew up with four female Aunts and six female cousins. I had several Great Aunts and - I don't even know how many - female second, third, and beyond, cousins. I have a fantastic Stepmother and four stepsisters – all female. I have a wonderful wife who is all Woman. I have a great sister-in-law who has a fabulous daughter, granddaughters and great-granddaughters. There are a lot of Women in my life who keep me in line and keep me going. Without them I wouldn't be around anymore. It is because of them and for them that I can write this book.

Why write this book, you may ask. I mean really, why does that question "What is a Woman?" need to be answered in the first place. You know, you'd think the answer would be obvious. Well, the other night I was lying in bed with my wife. It was after midnight. I had my hand on my wife's belly – she was sleeping. Thoughts were roiling around in my head and I was remembering some of the stories I had seen on the news in the past week – all of them concerning women in one way or another. What stuck in my head were the issues America – and a few other places – were having with transgenders in sports, all the LGBTQ2S+ stuff that was going on, and news stories concerning women in Afghanistan, when I remembered the statement by Judge Ketanji Brown Jackson that she couldn't define what a Woman was because she "wasn't a biologist."

Well, I am a biologist. That isn't my profession. I'm retired now, but I was a Commercial Diver – I even worked with Women in that field. Anyway, I earned a Bachelor of Science degree in Biology so that makes me somewhat of a Biologist – at least enough of one to answer the question: What is a Woman?

So here it is.

By the way, I don't mean to offend anyone by writing this book, it is just something I had to get off my chest. I hope you enjoy it in the very least and maybe it will even get you thinking about yourself and all the Women in your life.

What is a Woman?

On March 23, 2022, during the second day of the Senate Judiciary Committee hearing for nomination to the Supreme Court, U.S. Senator Marsha Blackburn (R-Tenn.) questioned Judge Ketanji Brown Jackson:

"Can you provide a definition for the word '***woman***'?"

Judge Ketanji Brown Jackson replied:

"No, I can't. Not in this context, I'm not a biologist."

> "I am Woman Phenomenally.
> Phenomenal Woman, that's me."
> — Maya Angelou

> "One of the best things that ever happened to me is that I'm a Woman.
> That is the way all Females should feel."
> — Marilyn Monroe

> "A Woman is the Full Circle.
> Within her is the Power to Create, Nurture, and Transform."
> — Diane Mariechild

> "I am Woman, Hear Me Roar!"
> — Helen Reddy

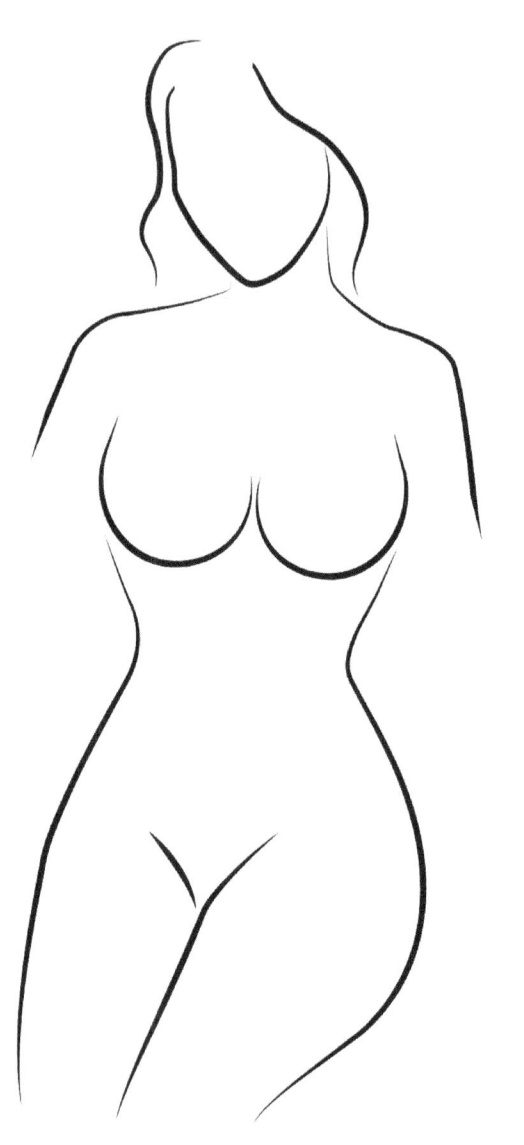

I

Biologically a Woman is:

If we open up any book on human biology there is going to be a definition of a woman in black and white – unless the book is published in other colors! We could go to the Glossary of said book and it will say something to the effect of: "A **Woman** is an adult **Female Human**." So then we may ask what is the definition of "**Female Human**?" In the Glossary we will find something like: "Belonging to the sex which conceives and gives birth to young, or (in a wider sense) which has an ovary and produces ova; not male."

With modern science we can get down to a simpler definition of what a Woman is biologically. We can get right down to the cellular structure and it is quite simple really. Genetically, human beings have 46 chromosomes - made up of hundreds or even thousands of genes - combined into 23 pairs (for the most part – of course there are variations but these do not determine gender). To get back to our task –

defining female – there is only one pair we are concerned with. That is the pair designated the number 23, but more commonly referred to as the "Sex Chromosomes." This pair is made up of two chromosomes: an X chromosome coming from the mother, and either an X or a Y chromosome coming from the father. The joining of the mother's Ovum with the father's Sperm forms a Zygote – a little single celled thing with 46 chromosomes that will develop into a human being if all goes well.

If the zygote's sex pair is XX the new life form is determined – by biology, not humans – to be a female. If the zygote's sex pair is XY then this new life form is determined – again by biology, not humans – to be a male. Occasionally the zygote will have an extra sex chromosome, 2 X's and 1 Y, forming an XXY situation. The extra X chromosome may come from either the father or the mother and is not a genetic trait passed down from one generation to the next. This is called Klinefelter Syndrome. Since the Y chromosome is present the zygote is male. Rarely an extra Y chromosome comes into play forming an XYY condition. This is Jacob's Syndrome. This zygote is also male because of the presence of a Y chromosome. Jacob's Syndrome is not passed down from one generation to the next either. There is also another combination of the sex chromosomes and that is the presence of 3 X chromosomes. This is called Trisomy or Triple X Syndrome. This zygote, of course, is female – because of the lack of a Y chromosome and, like the 2 previous conditions is not passed from one generation to the next.

So here we are, genetically there are only 2 genders: Female

– no Y chromosome is present - and Male – a Y chromosome is present.

But what about the *Intersex* condition!?! – in the past referred to as *Hermaphroditism* – I hear you screaming. Well, that is a different condition not necessarily determined by genetics. This is a condition medically referred to as **Ovotesticular Syndrome**. This is a condition where the body develops both male and female reproductive parts and other male/female traits in varying degrees. This is a developmental condition and not genetic. Most people with this condition are sterile, but not always, and contrary to popular belief they cannot impregnate themselves. I'm sure if one of you looks hard enough and delves into the internet deep enough you may find a case or two where this happened, but it is highly unlikely.

Even in the cases of people with the intersex condition, genetically they are either Female or Male. Their bodies will react to medications, hormones, and any medical treatment the way the XX human body or the XY human body will; determined by whether or not they have a Y chromosome.

I know this is hard or sad for some of you to learn, or admit to, but genetically speaking there are only 2 genders and a Woman is defined as being the one who is lacking the Y chromosome.

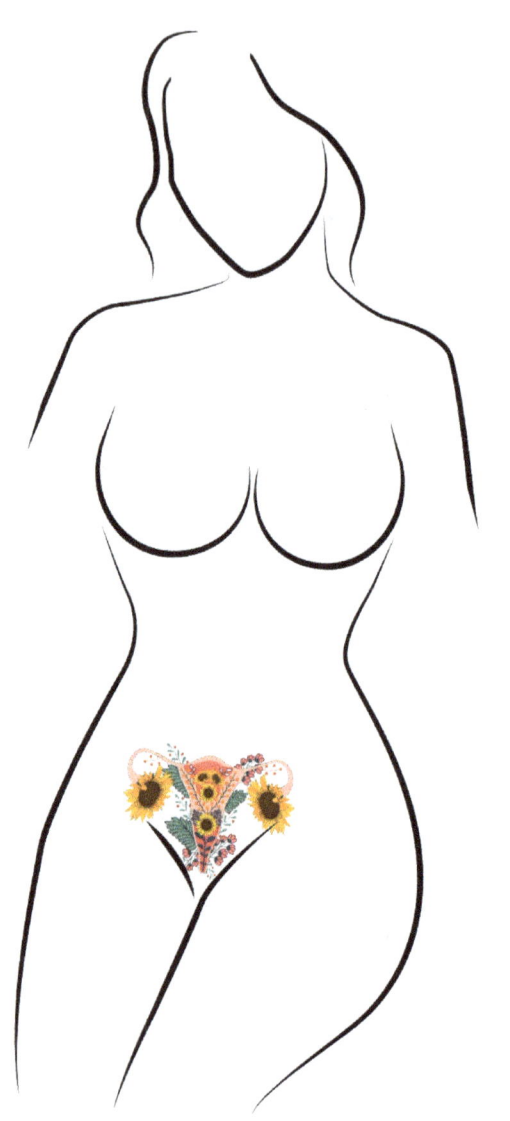

2

Physically a Woman is:

Wow! Where do I start with this one? Right off the bat, I'd say this is what we see when we look at a fellow human being. In the old days, if you were wearing a dress, you were seen as a Woman; wearing pants, you were seen as a man. Or in the real old days – like "Cave Man" days – if you had a Vulva and enlarged Breasts you were a Woman; if, on the other hand, you had a Penis you were a man. Seems simple enough, and maybe it was. That was before my time, though, so I don't really know.

These days things are not so simple. When I was a little kid growing up in America, if you had long hair and wore a dress you were a girl and if you had short hair and wore pants you were a boy. If you were a girl and liked running around in pants and playing with the boys you were a tomboy. When I was a little kid boys didn't wear dresses – except maybe on Hallowe'en – so there was no name for that. Until I got older and found out that some men did like to dress like women. Then they were called queer, or sometimes fairies, they weren't Women though.

When I was older I heard about and saw Queens – men dressed in "drag" and impersonating women. They do their best to look like women accentuating all the very most visual parts of being a woman. Many are not trying to be a real Woman, they are entertainers. It is their job to personify the most feminine women. I even saw once where Dolly Parton entered a Dolly Parton Look-alike Contest and lost to a Queen. What a success for that person! But Dolly was the real Woman, the female human being.

Now (and even when I was a little kid – I just didn't realize it) Women, and men, can wear their hair anyway they want, they can dress any way they want, and do whatever jobs they want. It is hard to tell just by looking whether your fellow human being is a Woman or a Man – not always, but sometimes. You can't always tell by talking to your fellow human being either. Some women have very deep voices and some men have very high voices. Neither of those are indicative of gender even though we normally associate the higher voice with Women and a lower voice with Men.

According to the dictionary a Woman is "an adult female human being." Remember a "female" is defined as "having Ovaries and producing an Ovum." That is more than just having a Vulva. In fact the Vulva isn't even mentioned in the definition of a Woman and neither is the Vagina. This brings me to the "Gender Affirmation" medical treatments. I know this is going to piss a lot of you off and I am sorry. I don't care one way or the other how you identify or how you want to dress or what you want to be, I don't think any less of you for your choices. You let me live my life, and I'll let you live yours. We are all human beings afterall.

We are just trying to define what a Woman is here. Just because you cut off all the maleness and add all the femaleness doesn't make you a Woman. The sad truth is that you can't introduce the Ovaries and the Uterus into the male human body, have them take hold and function like they do in a female body. There are just too many differences – as determined by genetics – between the body types to allow that to happen. By the same token; just because you cut off all the female parts and add all the male parts doesn't make you a man.

"If it looks like a duck, walks like a duck, and quacks like a duck, it must be a duck." Not necessarily so – it might be a Robot or a toy, or even a decoy. None of those are really ducks even if they look like ducks. Even though they look like women, are all those feminine sex dolls and robots really Women? Even the inflatable ones? I don't think so, and I don't think you think they are either.

Is a transgender woman really a Woman? I'm sorry to rain on your parade, but no, they are not. Every true Woman is a Woman on a cellular level – that is she has only X chromosomes and no Y chromosomes. Normally she has or has had Ovaries and a Uterus as well as the Vagina and Vulva. Her body will support those organs. A male body will not support those organs. So just because one looks like a Woman and sounds like a Woman doesn't make one a Woman. A transgender woman has no Ovaries, produces no Ova and has no Uterus in which to nurture a fertilized Ovum. Therefore, even though one may look like a Woman, sound like a Woman and even identify as a Woman she is not really a Woman.

A Woman, however, can present as whatever she wants but she is still a female. She can dress however she wants, do whatever she wants, call herself whatever she wants, remove whatever body parts she wants, add any other body parts she desires, but on a cellular level she still has no Y chromosome and is therefore still a female.

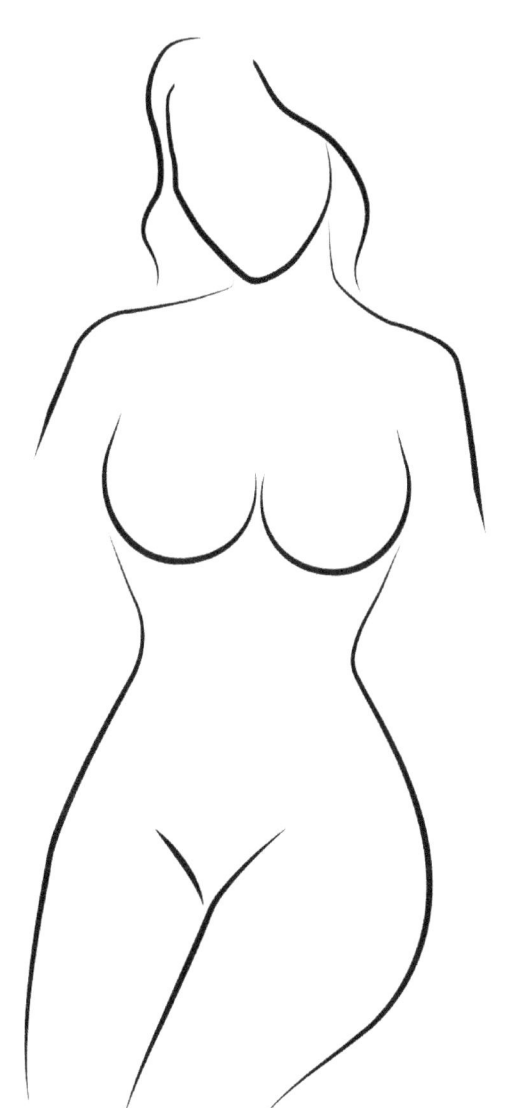

3

Psychologically a Woman is:

Psychologically a Woman is . . .

I don't know what a Woman is psychologically. Do you?

♀ ♀ ♀

4

But What is a Woman Really?

A Woman is something quite special. A Woman is a female human being who started out as an Ovum that got penetrated by a Spermatozoon carrying an X chromosome thereby becoming a Zygote. The Zygote turns into a Blastocyst after 4 days of cell division and then develops into an Embryo. After another 39 weeks or so the embryo has fully developed into a baby ready to be born (if everything has progressed along normally – we are not getting into variations here). Through all this the being has an XX genome – determining that she is a Female.

After being born a girl, this little bundle of joy will continue to grow and develop. She will go through all the wonderful times of being a child and also go through some hardships. All of these experiences will combine to make her the person she becomes. Somewhere between 8 and 13 years (on average) the girl goes through Puberty – that is, the reproductive organs in her body develop and mature into that of an adult female or a Woman. From here on out, no matter what we call her or how she identifies within herself, she is a Woman – an adult female human being.

Along with the development of her body comes the development of her brain. There are some innate traits of the female brain that differ from the male brain – what those are, we really don't know, but we do know that what we consider to be feminine thought is different than what we consider to be masculine thought on some levels. At least we tend to divide thoughts and actions to be either more feminine or more masculine. Personally, I think Human Beings think the way they do regardless of gender and there is not as much difference as society tries to point out.

I mean let's look at the activities we do and enjoy: Cooking for one – Masculine or Feminine? In public schools it is taught in Home Ec and generally considered to be a Feminine activity. How do you explain the male Chef then? Like Gordon Ramsay, Wolfgang Puck, or Ming Tsai? They are pretty manly men. How about shooting and hunting? There are many Women who are very good at it and enjoy it as much as men do. My wife is an excellent hunter and so is one of her nieces. Neither of them would be considered manly women, but they enjoy a sport normally associated as masculine. The examples go on and on – Fashion, Sports, Construction Work, Scientific Studies, Extreme Sports – all of those are enjoyed by human beings of both genders and have no relevance on how masculine or feminine the people are who enjoy those activities.

And colors – do colors or color preference denote gender? Of course not. Currently Americans associate Blue with Boys and Pink with Girls. Hah! What a laugh. Did you know that back in the late 1800s it was the other way around? Pink for Boys and Blue for Girls. Yeah, really. And all children wore dresses back then until they were three or four years old – it made it easier to change their diapers. How about Purple? That color used to be associated with Royalty – or Death – depending on what part of the world you lived in – but it had nothing to do with gender. We like what colors we like and those preferences have nothing to do with how feminine or masculine we are.

The point of all this is that I think our brains aren't that different for the most part. That is until you delve into the function and control of the body. Female hormones and reproductive functions are different than the Male's. There has to be some difference in the way the two brains function to account for those differences. We don't know very much about how the brain works in the first place, let alone what these small differences between the male and female brain might be. What I do know is that there is a magic in the female brain that makes the female body work and continue on with the nurturing and development of her offspring even into that offspring's maturity and beyond.

What is a woman really? She is special. She is really special. A woman is really special, that is what she really is.

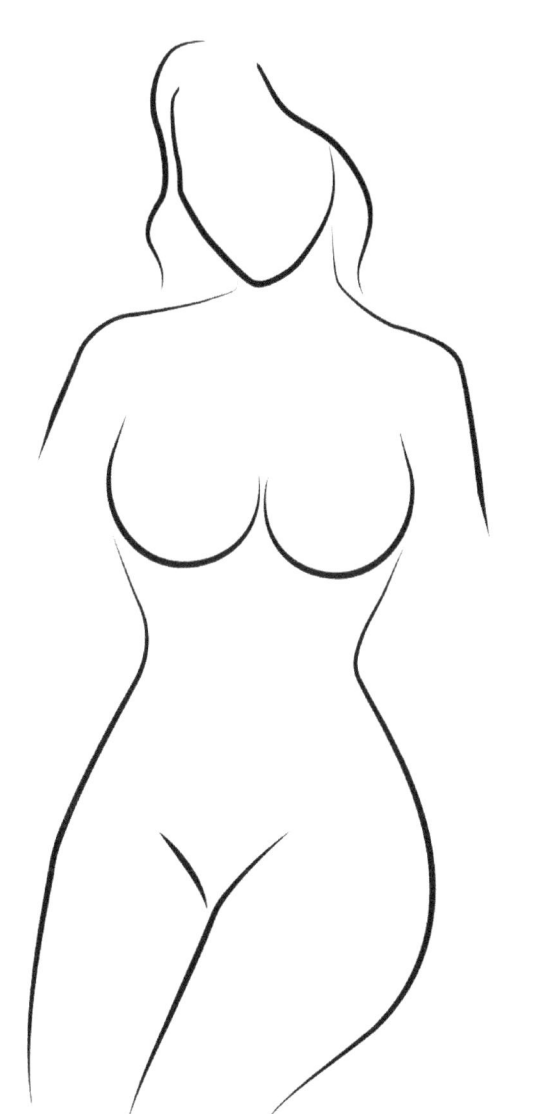

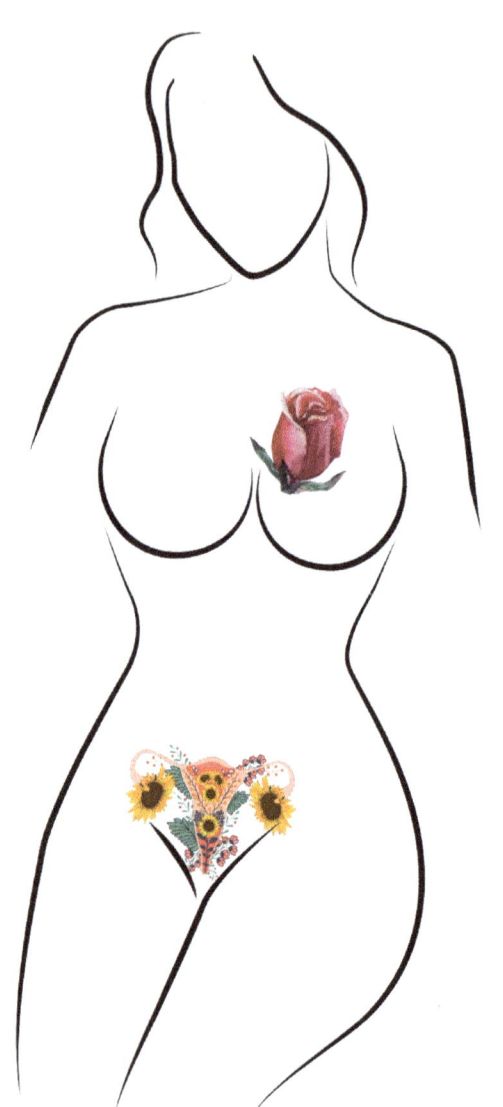

5

A Degree of Femininity

Sometimes a Woman can be very effeminate and other times she can be quite manly. Neither one of those states determines whether or not she is really a Woman. By the same token a man can be very manly or very effeminate – again, neither of those states determines how much of a male that person is.

Someone came up with a linear scale with 100% Maleness on one end and 100% Femaleness on the other end, stating that most of us fall somewhere in between those two extremes. I think that is somewhat on the right track, but I also think it is too 1-dimensional. I think the human psyche is more complex than that and more factors need to be taken into account.

For example, I think it is possible for a male to feel 100% female in every way, but since that person is a male he doesn't fit on the linear scale. In order to be 100% feminine like he feels, he would also have to be genetically female to reach the 100% female spot. The linear model doesn't really allow for intersex people either. Maybe we need a triangle – you know; one corner for 100% maleness, one for 100% femaleness, and the third for 100% intersexness. But what is 100% intersexness? How can we define that? I don't think we can. I think we need something more like a circle, but then I don't think a circle covers it either. Neither would a series of interconnected circles – those diagrams would always leave someone out.

I think it is more like a sphere; a cloud-filled sphere with the 100% Female as a polar opposite to the 100% Male. There is no top or bottom. I think we all fall somewhere within that sphere without being forced to be labeled as 100% male, 70% female, or 50% what? Male and Female? You can locate yourself anywhere on the outside of that sphere as well as anywhere in the middle of the sphere floating in the cloud somewhere. The linear labels just don't work. I see a sphere-shaped cloud of all different colors and each of us falls somewhere in that space as some sort of mixture of feelings and instincts; human, animal, male, and female. I also think our spot in that cloud changes as we go through our lives, experiencing new things, growing and changing as we mature and age, ultimately approaching death.

I know I don't fit onto a linear graph. I am 100% sexually attracted to females. Even though I like super-effeminate women who like to wear dresses and frilly lingerie, I also like women in tight jeans, button-up shirts, and cowboy boots. That doesn't mean I can't look at a man and see why he is attractive to women. I have an earring, my favorite color is purple, and I like to wear frilly shirts – like the royals did in the 17th and 18th centuries. That doesn't make me necessarily effeminate. It just adds to who I am. I think everybody is like that.

I think we should embrace those differences between us and accept those differences. I don't think we should force our beliefs, likes, and dislikes on others though. It used to be harder to be ourselves, because it seems that people used to be more judgemental than we are now. I don't think we were individually more judgemental, but society as a whole was more judgemental – less accepting of differences. I think it's better now, but I also think we need to drop the labels. It seems to me that the labeling is worse than it was before. If you were born a male, you are a male. If you were born a female, you are a female. If you were born intersex, you are intersex, genetically you are still only male or female. That's all there is to it. You can't become a Woman by wearing a woman's skin. You can't become a man by wearing a man's skin. Just like you can't become a bear by wearing a bearsuit, or a cat by wearing a catsuit, or whatever.

Changing your gender on your Identification just because you "identify" as something different is stupid. If you are in an accident, or some sort of life-threatening situation, your treatment may depend on what your genetic gender is and if you are mislabeled on your identification you may end up in worse shape than if the medical personnel knew what your real gender is. I feel the same way about gender affirmation surgery. It doesn't bother me that you want to live your life as a different gender than what you were born, but medically it is stupid to try to force your body to change genders. You are just asking for more troubles medically the older you get. For women who want to become men, your body still produces female hormones. It is hard enough on a female when she goes through menopause with all the changing hormones. You want to add to that by having all those extra male hormones in your body, when your body is trying to figure out how to keep itself healthy? You can't really change it anyway. Your cells are still either female – lacking a Y chromosome, or male – having a Y chromosome.

Gender affirmation surgery on young people who haven't even developed yet is even worse. A growing body is going through all kinds of changes – the hormones go crazy during puberty and it continues until the human body is about 25 years old. You don't realize the damage you are doing to that changing body and what problems you will have later in life resulting from all that messing around. You think the doctors performing those surgeries care about that? They don't. They care about the money they are making, or the status they get from performing however many "successful" operations they do. You think they will be around in 10 or 20 years when you really start to have health problems? Don't make me laugh. Have a little respect for your body and yourself. Dress however you want, identify however you want, but take care of yourself and don't damage or destroy your body on purpose.

I identify as a pegleg pirate with only one eye and a hook for a hand. I think I'll go to a doctor and ask to have my leg removed, my hand cut off, and my eye poked out. Yeah, that's a good idea. Are you kidding me? Think about it. Think about yourself in the long run. Take care of yourself.

I know many of you disagree with me and that's okay. We are all entitled to our own opinions. I think if you are comfortable wearing whatever clothing and body parts you want, fine, do it. Don't get upset at other people for using what you consider to be improper pronouns though. That's just silly. I used to have a big blond afro and several times when people came up behind me, they thought I was a woman and called me "ma'am," only to see me as a man with a beard when I turned around. That never upset me. Most often I think they were embarrassed by their mistake. I would never correct them, because it didn't matter. The Universe could care less what pronoun is used, why should I care? Why should you?

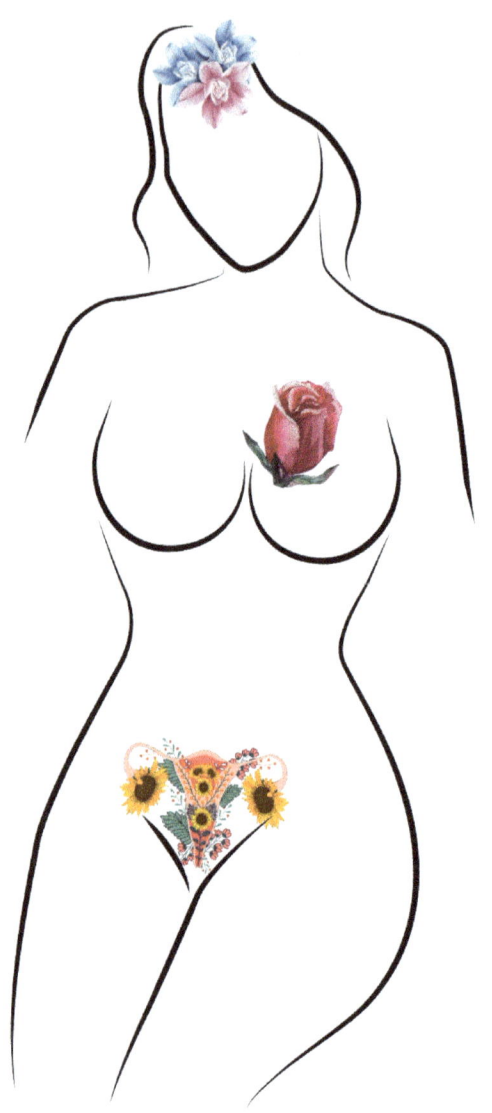

6

A Woman is Magic

So far we have mostly been talking about what a Woman is not, or more precisely, what is not a Woman. By now though we know what a Woman is according to biology. What a woman really is though is Magic. Why she is magic is because of Biology – shocking, I know. Smiles. Let me tell you How she is Magic.

First of all, she is Magic because she can produce children. Oh, but she can't do that without men you say, but the truth of the matter is that she can. It's easiest and most simple – let alone the way it is supposed to be done – if both the male and the female are involved. That is what helps with genetic diversity and genetic diversity is what helps our species survive in a changing world. The whole purpose of sexual reproduction – versus asexual (without sex) reproduction – is genetic diversity. But Women can reproduce without men by having their Ovum (egg) fertilized without a male. Okay, yes in that situation they need a male donor, but they don't need the male.

Without the use of a male donor, the egg can be implanted with the nucleus from some other human cell – that would be cloning. You don't need a male to clone, you can clone females all day long. What you do need is an Ovum and who produces those? Women of course! Yes, I know, human beings have not yet been cloned, but that doesn't mean it isn't possible. So far scientists have successfully cloned sheep – remember Dolly? (no, not Dolly Parton! Sheesh!) Dolly the Sheep – she was cloned by scientists in Scotland. Lots of animals have been cloned since Dolly: fruit flies, frogs, cats, dogs, pigs, goats, and even large animals like cattle, camels, and horses. There are more, but you can look them up as easily as I can if you are really interested.

Back to how Women are Magic. They can produce Ova. That in itself is the most magical thing in the universe, I think. Only Women can do that. There are two main parts of their bodies that make them magic and those are their reproductive organs, consisting of the Ovaries, Uterus, Vagina and Vulva, and their brain. How these organs function together is the way the female works her magic. Let me explain.

First is the Ovaries. They produce the Ova (the eggs) and get them ready for fertilization. That egg flows down one of the fallopian tubes until it reaches the Uterus where it waits to be fertilized. The Vulva is the entrance to the Vaginal area. It is what protects the Vagina and ultimately the Uterus from environmental hazards, but also allows the reproductive material (sperm – usually supplied by a willing male) to enter the vaginal passage and make its way to the egg waiting to be fertilized. The Vagina, or vaginal passage, is a tunnel of muscle and fiber that the female body uses to help extract genetic material from the male donor. The Vagina also guides this genetic material towards the Uterus. At the end of the vaginal passage is the Cervix. The Cervix functions as a gate between the Vagina and the Uterus. It helps keep germs and other material out of the Uterus, but also allows the sperm to enter and fertilize the waiting egg. Once the egg is fertilized it attaches to the uterine wall.

At this point the fertilized egg – now called a Zygote – starts to divide and develop into an embryo and from there into a little baby. The female body undergoes some changes that facilitate the growing baby. When the baby is fully developed – after 40 weeks – the Uterus and Vagina all work together with the brain to allow the birthing of the new baby. After the baby is born, the female body gets itself back in order and ready to go through the same magical process again.

The female brain is also part of what makes a woman magic in many ways. One way, in the unconscious control of all the functions of the female body and coordinating the actions of the individual organs to keep the body alive as well as prepare it for reproduction. When the female brain finds an attractive mate, it does what is needed by making the female attractive to the male counterpart. Both the conscious and unconscious parts of the brain work together with the rest of her body to get the female pregnant.

After the child is born, the female body produces food for the infant. I think on average the child will breastfeed for 6 months to a year. The female body will produce milk for much longer if it is healthy and perceives a need for producing milk longer – I have heard of women nursing their child to the age of 5.

The female brain also has a huge capacity for love and caring. Many women have the urge or the need to care for others around them. This includes their mates, their children, pets, and their extended family and friends. They have the desire to provide a home and prepare food for those they care for. They also feel the need to take care of any medical issues their loved ones may have – whether that is just the removal of a splinter or cleaning and bandaging of a small wound all the way to long term care for their parents, spouses, and others.

When I look at a Woman, I can't help but see how magic they are and what they and their bodies are capable of. When I lay my hand on my wife's tummy, I can feel the magic emanating from that part of her body. When I touch my forehead to hers, I can sense the magic emanating from her brain. It amazes me every day.

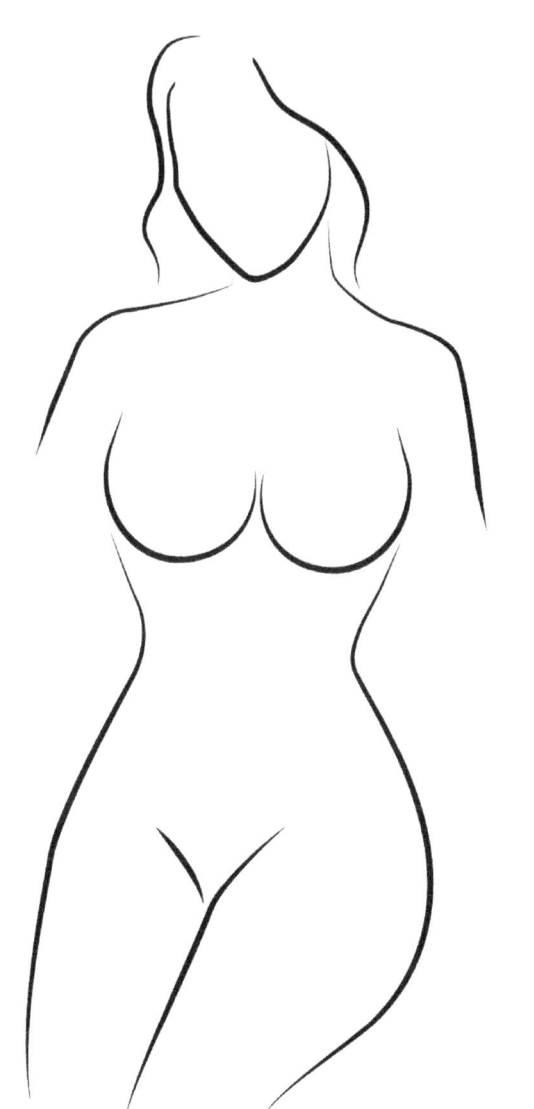

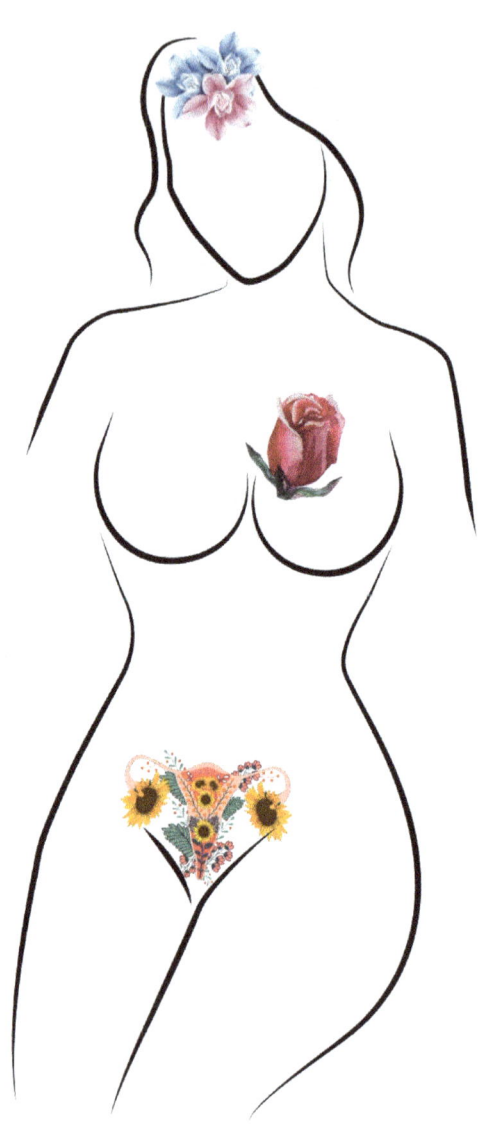

Epilogue

As I lay in bed, after midnight, with my hand on my wife's tummy and all those questions and thoughts in my head, I feel something emanating from my wife's Ovaries and Uterus. I lean my head into her head, my temple touching her temple, and I sense something emanating from her brain. It is warm. It is powerful. It is an energy. It is an energy that engulfs me, takes me away, and protects me. I listen to her breathing. I watch her chest rise and fall slowly with each breath. I feel myself become enveloped by her strength and being. Then I realize I know the answer to that question: What is a Woman? You know what a Woman is? A Woman is Magic. That's what a Woman is. Magic.

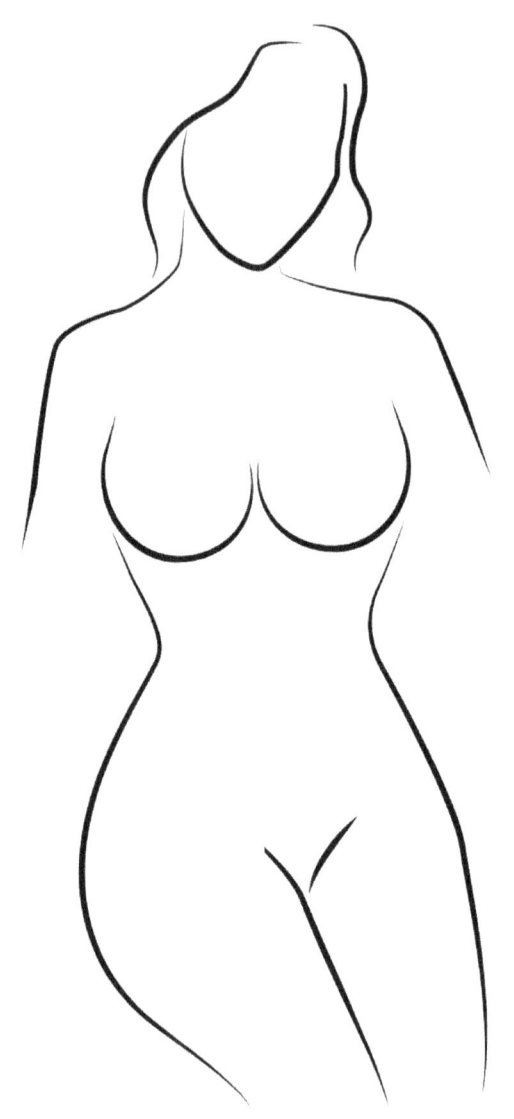

"God gave women intuition and femininity.
Used properly, the combination easily
jumbles the brain of any man I've ever met."
Farrah Fawcett

"Woman is the dominant sex.
Men have to do all sorts of stuff to prove
that they are worthy of woman's attention."
Camille Paglia

"I feel there is something unexplored about
Woman that only a
Woman can explore."
Georgia O'Keeffe

"Some of us are becoming
the men we wanted to marry."
Gloria Steinem

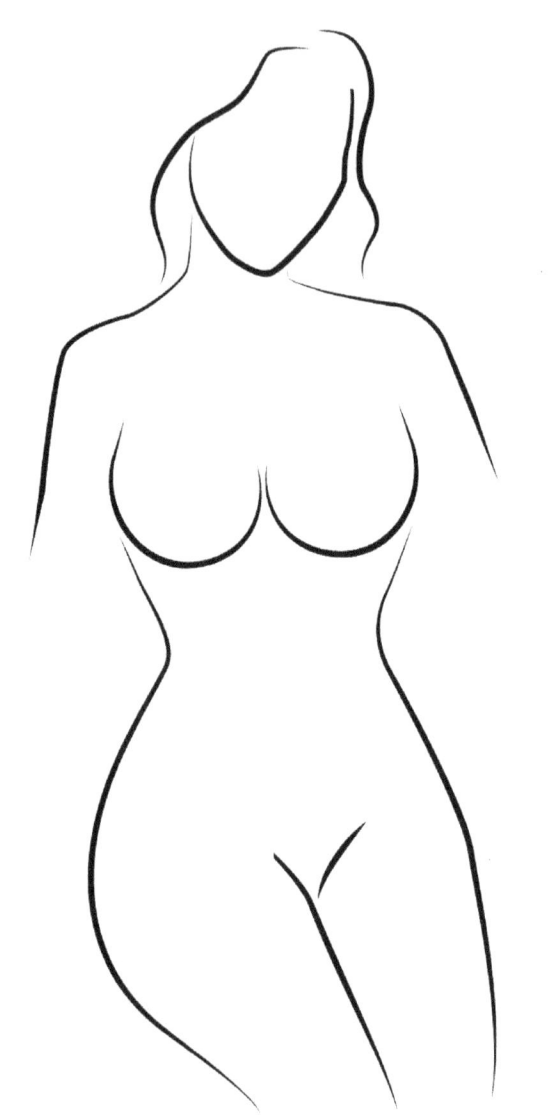

"Women are the real architects of society."
Cher

"I do not wish women to have power over men; but over themselves."
Mary Shelley

"It may be the cock that crows, but it is the hen that lays the eggs."
Margaret Thatcher

"I am a woman and a warrior. If you think I can't be both, you've been lied to."
Jennifer Zeynab Joukhadar

"After women, flowers are the most lovely thing God has given the world."
Christian Dior

Acknowledgements

I would like to thank my mother for bringing me into this world in the first place - she did it with my father's help.

I would like to thank all 3 of my sisters for helping me grow up and introducing me to female issues.

I would especially like to thank my sister, Heather, for being the Ray of Sunshine in many people's lives.

I would like to thank the mother of my children for helping me bring 2 wonderful children into my life.

I would like to thank my wife, Cindy, who has helped me beyond measure.

I would like to thank my daughter, Anarachel, for letting me experience the joy and wonder of being allowed to help raise a daughter.

I would like to thank All the Women I have encountered in my life for helping me experience life.

About the Author

sam humphrey

Sam lives in Helena, Montana with his lovely and hard-working wife, Cindy, and their two cats, Spook and Boo. He spends his time reading, writing, doing craft projects and puzzles. He enjoys a good game of Backgammon or Chess when he can find someone to play. He also enjoys playing Scrabble, Boggle, and Cribbage with his wife, Cindy. Sam also enjoys the time he gets to spend with the women in his life.

Other Books by sam

What the HELL Happened to Me?

    My physical and mental struggles after a catastrophic motorcycle accident and ending up a paraplegic in a wheelchair, Cindy's absolute dedication and her unwavering devotion, my family and friend's loving support, the skills and patience of most of the staff I have had in the various medical facilities - it all adds up to one stunning story of horrible luck, remarkable resilience and a heart warming relationship that binds it all together.

WET PAY:
Stories from my Career as a Commercial Diver

    A semi-biographical collection of stories told from my point of view. These are funny, exciting, and sometimes horrifying true tales of my experiences working above and below the surface of the water. The jobs were on dams, bridges, in rivers, lakes and the oceans.

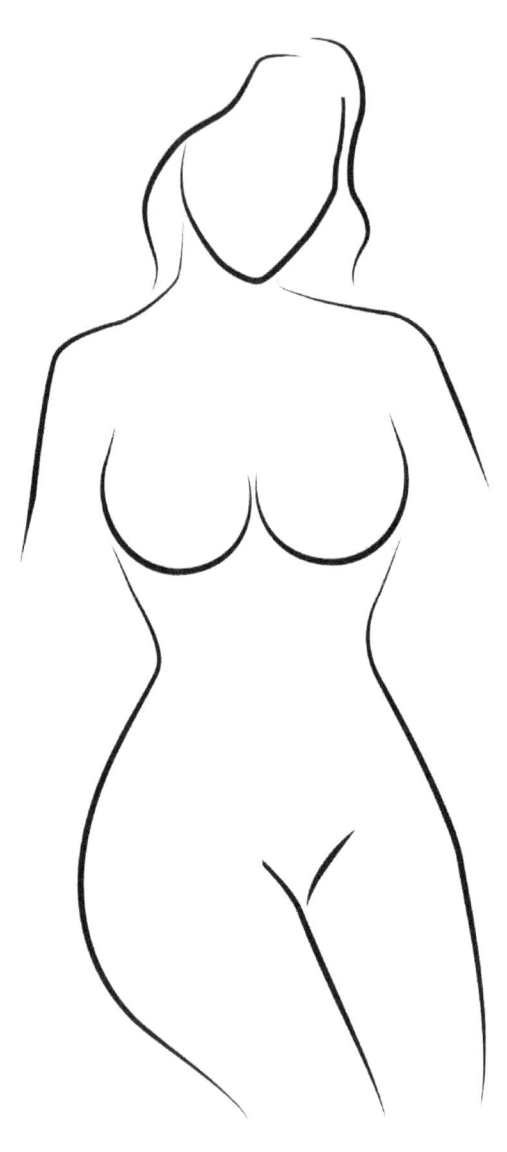

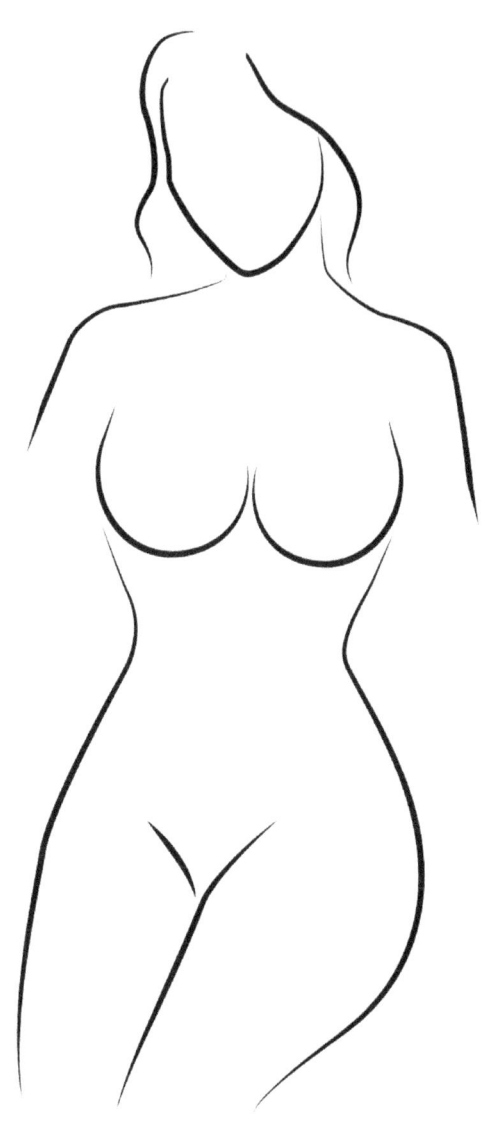

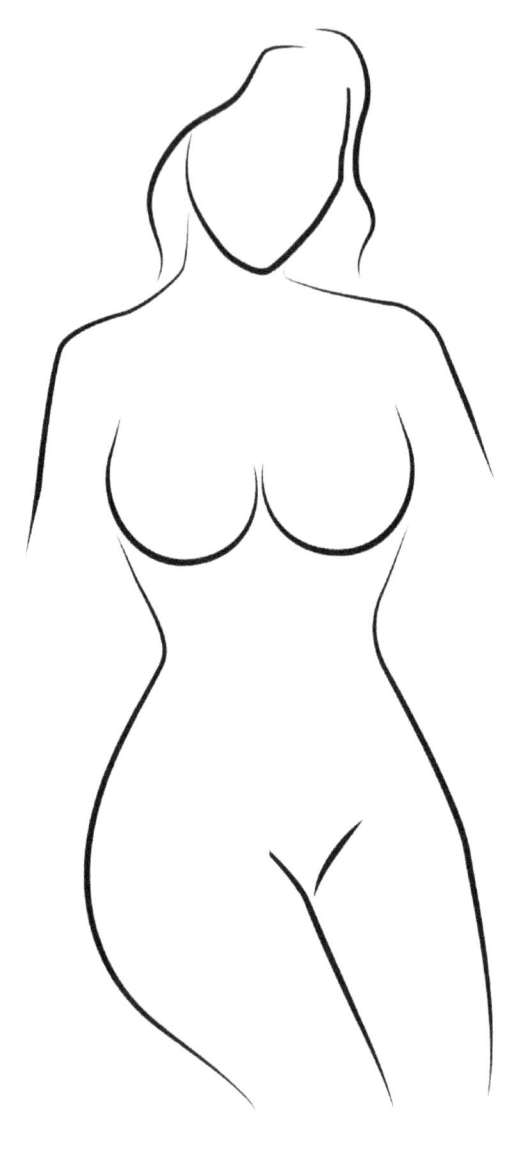

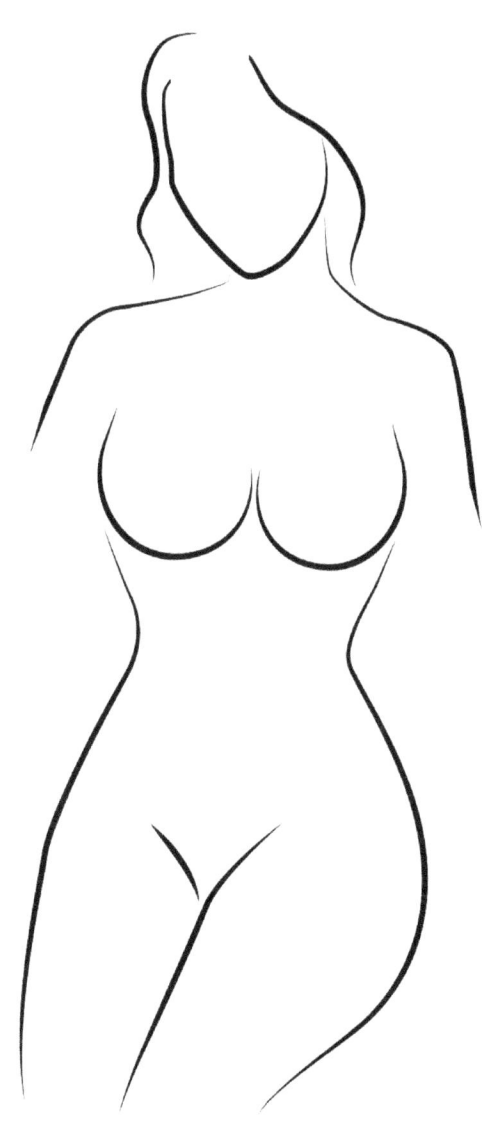

www.ingramcontent.com/pod-product-compliance
Lightning Source LLC
Chambersburg PA
CBHW070241010526
44107CB00041B/1479/J